7.6 BILLION PEOPLE LIVING IN THE COUNTRIES OF THE WORLD

BEN HUBBARD

W
FRANKLIN WATTS
LONDON • SYDNEY

First published in Great Britain in 2018 by
The Watts Publishing Group
Copyright © The Watts Publishing
Group 2018

Editor: Julia Bird/Julia Adams
Design and illustration: Mark Ruffle
www.rufflebrothers.com

ISBN: 978 1 4451 6083 2

Photo credits: Alchetron: 18b. Aphelleon/
Shutterstock: front cover tr. Richie Chan/Shutterstock:
8bc. Jonathan Chancasana/Shutterstock: 20cl.
Cathy Withers-Clarke/Shutterstock: 13tl. EcoPrint/
Shutterstock: 13c. f11photo/Shutterstock: 8bl.
F1online digitale Bildagentur GmbH/Alamy: 26b.
Stanislav Fosenbauer/Shutterstock: 23br. Ghost Bear/
Shutterstock: 15bc. Volodymyr Goinyk/Shutterstock:
front cover c. Anton Ivanov/Shutterstock: 20cr.
kakteen/Shutterstock: 19cr. Jess Kraft/Shutterstock:
front cover b. leoks/Shutterstock: 27b. Viacheslav
Lopatin/Shutterstock: 25b. Magdanatka/
Shutterstock: 13br. Maggie Meyer/Shutterstock:
13bl. Onyx9/Shutterstock: 13tr. Patrick Foto/
Shutterstock: 8br. Spencer Platt/Getty Images: 10b.
posztos/Shutterstock: 17bl. Saurav022/Shutterstock:
9b. sladkozaponi/Shutterstock: 5b. sumikophoto/
Shutterstock: 15bl. Trentinness/Dreamstime: 29t.
Xiong Wai/Shutterstock: 20c. wayak/Shutterstock:
18c. E White/CC Wikimedia Commons: 29b. Yuri
Yavnik/Shutterstock: 6b.

Franklin Watts
An imprint of
Hachette Children's Group
Part of The Watts Publishing Group
Carmelite House
50 Victoria Embankment
London EC4Y 0DZ

An Hachette UK Company
www.hachette.co.uk
www.franklinwatts.co.uk

MIX
Paper from
responsible sources
FSC® C104740
FSC
www.fsc.org

Printed in Dubai

Throughout the book you are given data relating
to various pieces of information covering the topic.
The numbers will most likely be an estimation based
on research made over a period of time and in a
particular area. Some other research may reach
a different set of data, and all these figures may
change with time as new research and information is
gathered. The numbers provided within this book are
believed to be correct at the time of printing and have
been sourced from the following sites:

UN, Worldbank, Britannica, CIA Factbook, Economist
World Figures, World Health Organisation, The
Lancet, NASA, National Geographic, Britannica,
The Smithsonian, European Space Agency, World
Economic Forum, European Group on Museum
Statistics, Motion Picture Association of America,
National Geographic Society, National Oceanic and
Atmospheric Association, World Shipping Council,
Archaeological Institute of America, World Wildlife
Foundation, TIME magazine, Statistical Yearbook of
Mexican cinema.

COUNTING COUNTRIES

Countries can be counted down by their size, or the number of their populations. They can also be counted down by their number of rivers, or bicycles. Whichever way they are counted down, here are some of the ways these countries are number one.

1. Russia is the largest country in the world, covering **17,100,000 sq km**.

2. Indonesia is the biggest producer of vegetable oil at **32,000,000 tonnes a year**.

3. India has the highest number of daily newspaper readers at **285,000,000 people**.

4. La Paz, Bolivia, is the highest capital city in the world at an altitude of **3,600 m**.

5. The United States of America has produced the most Nobel prize winners at 371.

6. Bermuda has the highest percentage of internet users with **98% of people online**.

7. Monaco has the highest life expectancy, with people living to an average age of **89**.

8. Uganda has the most young people: **68%** of its population are under **24**.

9. Rwanda has the highest percentage of woman in parliament at **61.3%**.

10. Guinea has the world's largest households, with an average of **8.6 people**.

BILLIONS OF PEOPLE IN THE WORLD

There are **7,600,000,000 people** living in the world's countries. That figure is rising by around **140 people** every minute. The world's population is predicted to reach **8.5 billion** by 2030 and **9.8 billion** by 2050.

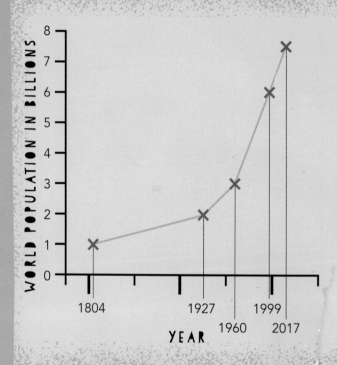

The crowded streets of Mumbai, India. The country is predicted to have the highest population in the world by 2022 with around **1.4 billion people**.

The countries of Asia are among the biggest in the world. Much of the land is uninhabited, and yet Asia's **48 countries** are home to **4,523,266,485 people**. That's more than half the world's population.

The people of Asia make up **59.77%** of the world's population.

ASIA

REST OF THE WORLD

EUROPE

ASIA

China

AFRICA

Great Wall of China

CHINA

If it was completely intact, the Great Wall of China would stretch half-way around the Earth.

ANCIENT DYNASTY

China is Asia's largest country at **9,572,900 sq km**. It also contains the highest population of any country in the world at **1,379,302,771 people**. Over **90%** of the population is descended from the Han people who settled in China over **5,000 years ago**. The Han Dynasty built the longest section of the Great Wall of China. The Great Wall stretches across a total distance of **21,196 km**.

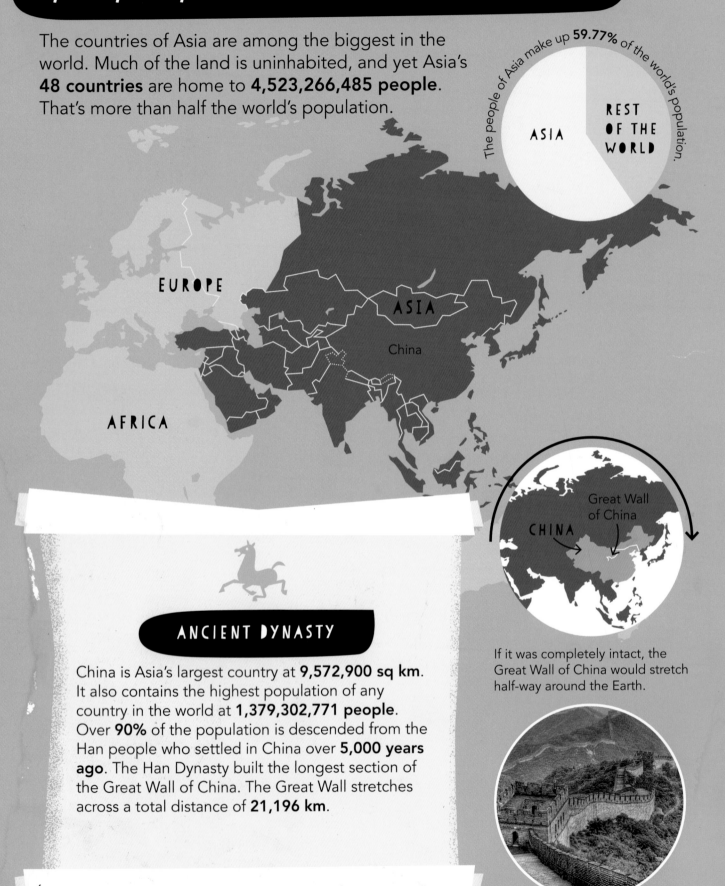

India is the second largest country in Asia. It also has the second highest population in the world at **1,346,060,715 people**.

USA: 5%

India: 18%

China: 19%

Rest of world 58%

After China and India, the USA has the third highest population the world at **326,625,791 people**.

OVER 422,048,642 INDIANS SPEAK HINDI

OVER 266,449,000 INDIANS SPEAK ENGLISH

INDIAN LANGUAGES

India has more languages than any other country, with over **1,000** spoken. The six main Indian languages are Hindi, English, Bengali, Telugu, Marathi, Tamil and Urdu.

OVER 83,369,769 INDIANS SPEAK BENGALI

OVER 74,002,856 INDIANS SPEAK TELUGU

FOOD PRODUCER

China and India are among the world's biggest exporters of food. Crops grown on Chinese soil feeds around **20%** of the world's population. Rice is one of the main crops grown across Asia.

145 104

36 34 27 16 12 11 8

Million tonnes of rice

China India Indonesia Vietnam Myanmar Japan
Bangladesh Thailand Philippines

The top **nine countries** in the world that export rice are all in Asia.

TOKYO IS THE LARGEST MEGACITY WITH 38,100,000 RESIDENTS

Over half of the world's population lives in cities. In Asia, **53%** of people are city-dwellers. Asian cities are among the most populated and fastest-growing in the world.

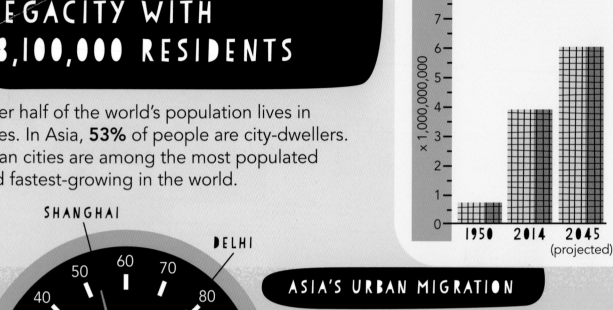

URBAN GROWTH WORLDWIDE

× 1,000,000,000

1950　2014　2045 (projected)

SHANGHAI

DELHI

50　60　70

40　80

30　90

20　100

10　120

0　130

PEOPLE PER HOUR

ASIA'S URBAN MIGRATION

China and India have rapidly growing economies. As their economies expand, people move from the countryside to the cities to work. This is called urban migration. Between 2001 and 2010, almost **200 million people** in Asia migrated from rural to urban centres. Today, Delhi in India is growing by **79 people per hour** and Shanghai in China by **53 people per hour**.

MEGACITIES

Megacities are cities with populations of over **10 million people**. Today there are **28 megacities**, the **three largest** of which are in Asia.

Tokyo, Japan: **38,100,000 people**

Delhi, India: **26,500,000 people**

Shanghai, China: **24,500,000 people**

JAPANESE GIANT

Tokyo in Japan was already a megacity by 1975. Its population then was **27 million**; today it is **38 million**. Over **94%** of Japan's population lives in the country's cities.

■ TOKYO URBAN SPRAWL 1972   ■ TOKYO TODAY

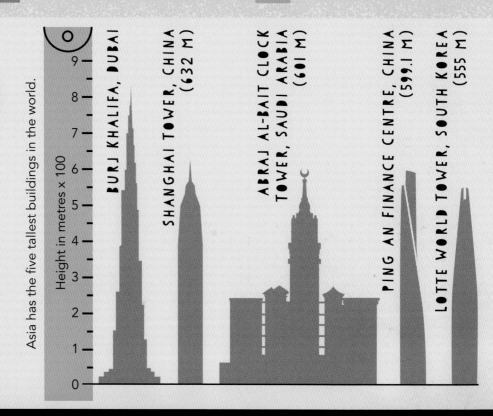

Height in metres x 100

Asia has the five tallest buildings in the world.

9 —
8 —
7 —
6 —
5 —
4 —
3 —
2 —
1 —
0 —

BURJ KHALIFA, DUBAI

SHANGHAI TOWER, CHINA (632 M)

ABRAJ AL-BAIT CLOCK TOWER, SAUDI ARABIA (601 M)

PING AN FINANCE CENTRE, CHINA (599.1 M)

LOTTE WORLD TOWER, SOUTH KOREA (555 M)

TALLEST TOWER

Asia is home to the world's tallest building: the Burj Khalifa in Dubai, United Arab Emirates. The building is **828.8 m high**, has **163 floors** and **57 elevators**. The elevators travel at **10 m per second**.

CITY POLLUTION

A consequence of economic growth in Asia's cities is pollution. In Delhi, India, in 2017, doctors declared a medical emergency after pollution levels reached **30 times** the safe limit. High levels of choking smog in the air made many people sick.

24,668,091 DIAMOND CARATS MINED IN BOTSWANA

Botswana is the **second** leading producer of diamonds in the world. It is one of Africa's **54 countries**, many of which are rich in mineral resources such as diamonds, gold and oil. Around **30%** of the Earth's remaining mineral resources are believed to lie in Africa.

COUNTING CARATS

Diamonds are measured in carats, which calculates their weight. Botswana produces **35%** of Africa's diamonds, which is around **24,668,091 diamond carats** every year. It is believed Botswana has **150 million carats** of diamonds left in its **four mines**, which will take until 2050 to be extracted.

RICH BUT POOR

Although many African countries are rich in resources, they are among the poorest countries in the world. Sometimes resources such as diamonds can lead to civil war, when illegal military groups seize control of diamond mines and use the money to fight wars with the government. Civil wars paid for with 'blood diamonds' have been fought in **seven** African countries and have cost around **3.7 million lives**.

In 2015, the world's **second biggest** diamond was discovered in Botswana's Karowe mine. The **1,109-carat** diamond sold for **US$53 million**. The biggest diamond ever found weighed in at **3,106 carats**. It was discovered in South Africa in 1905.

1,109-CARAT

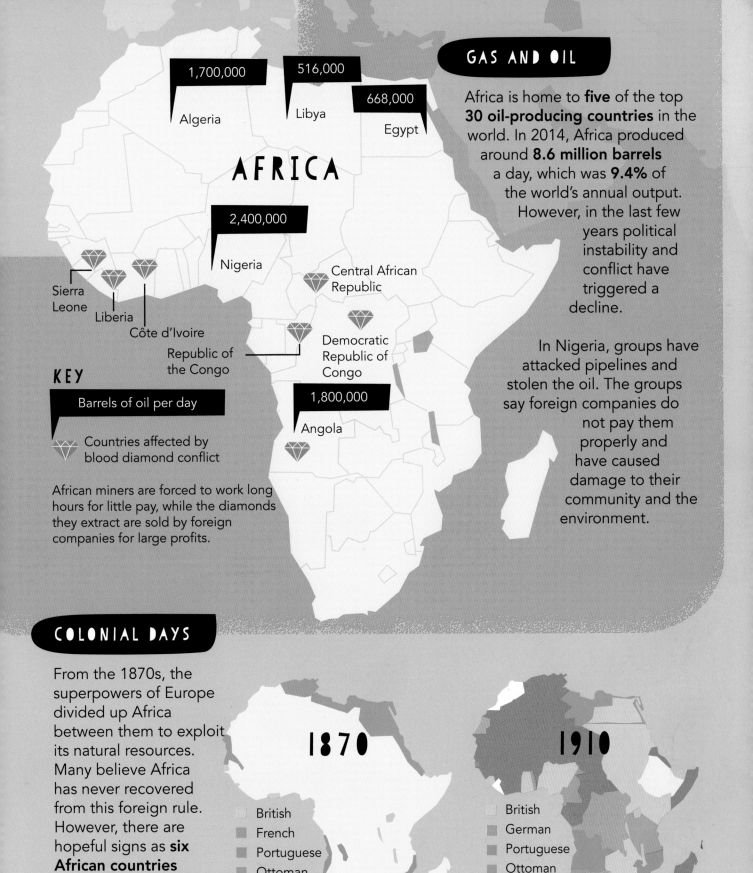

1,700,000

Algeria

516,000

Libya

668,000

Egypt

AFRICA

2,400,000

Nigeria

Central African Republic

Sierra Leone

Liberia

Côte d'Ivoire

Republic of the Congo

Democratic Republic of Congo

1,800,000

Angola

KEY

Barrels of oil per day

Countries affected by blood diamond conflict

African miners are forced to work long hours for little pay, while the diamonds they extract are sold by foreign companies for large profits.

GAS AND OIL

Africa is home to **five** of the top **30 oil-producing countries** in the world. In 2014, Africa produced around **8.6 million barrels** a day, which was **9.4%** of the world's annual output. However, in the last few years political instability and conflict have triggered a decline.

In Nigeria, groups have attacked pipelines and stolen the oil. The groups say foreign companies do not pay them properly and have caused damage to their community and the environment.

COLONIAL DAYS

From the 1870s, the superpowers of Europe divided up Africa between them to exploit its natural resources. Many believe Africa has never recovered from this foreign rule. However, there are hopeful signs as **six African countries** are today among the world's **ten fastest growing economies**.

1870

British
French
Portuguese
Ottoman
Dutch

1910

British
German
Portuguese
Ottoman
French
Spanish
Italian
Belgian

11

OVER 1,500,000 WILDEBEEST MIGRATE ANNUALLY FROM TANZANIA

Africa is home to many wild animals that roam free across its plains. Large animals weighing over **40 kg** are known as 'megafauna'. Africa has the highest number of megafauna species in the world.

AFRICAN MEGAFAUNA

HUMAN
Weight: 70 kg
Height: 1.7 m
Conservation status: low risk

GIRAFFE
Weight: 1,300 kg
Height: 5.5 m
Conservation status: vulnerable

WESTERN BLACK RHINO
Weight: 1,200 kg
Height: 1.6 m
Length: 3.5 m
Conservation status: extinct, 2011

AFRICAN BUSH ELEPHANT
Weight: 10,000 kg
Height: 3.9 m
Length: 6 m
Conservation status: vulnerable

AFRICA

Kenya

Tanzania

Serengeti National Park

THE GREAT MIGRATION

Every year, **1,500,000 wildebeest** and **200,000 zebras** migrate across northern Tanzania and Kenya. The mammals travel for around **1,931 km** through the countries' Serengeti National Park in search of greener pastures to graze on.

Illegal hunting, or poaching, in Tanzania is worth around **US$50 million** a year. It is not the only African country where poaching takes place. Many endangered animals are killed by poachers who sell a single part of their body, such as an elephant's tusks. Many of the animals that are hunted illegally are now endangered.

MOUNTAIN GORILLA: Fewer than **1,000** remain

BLACK RHINO: Population has dropped by **97.6%** since 1960

AFRICAN ELEPHANT: **35,000** killed in 2016

AFRICAN LION: Extinct in **26** African countries

GREVY'S ZEBRA: Only **2,000** adults remain

BIRDS AND FISH

Africa's animals also include an abundance of birds, fish, insects and reptiles. There are over **3,000 species of freshwater fish** in Africa, more than any other continent. Over **2,600 species of bird** are at home here, too.

Over **760 species** of dragonfly live in Africa.

African black mambas are aggressive, highly venomous snakes that can move at **20 km/h** and inject lethal venom with their **22 mm-long** fangs.

CANADA'S COASTLINE STRETCHES FOR 202,080 KM

Many record-breaking physical features and landmarks make up the **24.7 million square km** of North America. In the north are huge lakes, frozen tundra and the Arctic circle. In the south are hot deserts, massive plains and lush rainforests.

Canada has the world's longest coastline at **202,080 km.** If straightened out, it could wrap around the Earth **five times.**

x5

Canada's border with the United States of America stretches for **8,891 km** and is the longest border between two countries.

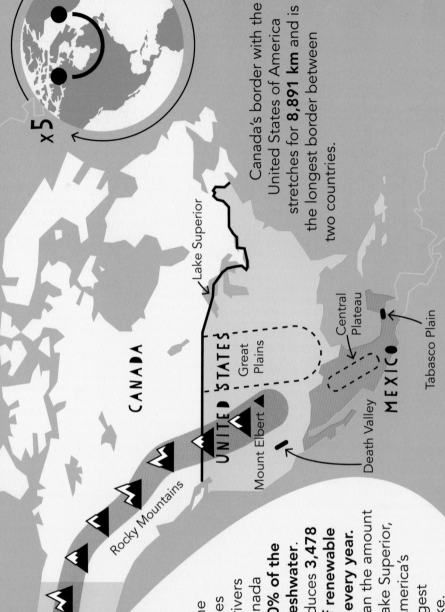

CANADA

UNITED STATES

Mount Elbert

Great Plains

Rocky Mountains

Lake Superior

MEXICO

Central Plateau

Death Valley

Tabasco Plain

The lakes and rivers of Canada contain **20% of the world's freshwater.** Canada produces **3,478 cubic km of renewable freshwater every year.** That's more than the amount of water in Lake Superior, North America's biggest lake.

CANADA

Canada is the largest country in North America, covering **9,984,670 sq km.** That's over **three times bigger** than India.

x3

MEXICO

Mexico covers **1,972,550 sq km** of North America and shares a **3,140-km border** with the USA. Mexico has **two mountain ranges** running through it: the Sierra Madre Oriental and the Sierra Madre Occidental. In between lies the country's heavily populated Central Plateau.

Mexico's Tabasco Plain is a **24,000 sq km** area of tropical rainforest. It has the widest variety of life in North America, which includes snakes, monkeys, puma, anteaters and **520 species of bird.**

The Sonoran, Mojave and Chihuahuan are the **three of the major deserts** lying across the southern USA and northern Mexico. The deserts experience an annual rainfall of **10–20 cm a year.** Only hardy plants like the acacia tree can grow there.

Acacia tree

UNITED STATES

The United States of America is the second largest country in North America at **9,800,000 sq km.** It features the lowest point on the continent: Death Valley, which is **86 m** below sea level. Death Valley is also North America's hottest place with a scorching **56.7 C** recorded there.

5 6.7°

The USA's Grand Canyon is the largest gorge in the world. It is **477 km** long and up to **29 km wide.** The canyon was formed around **five million years ago.**

MOUNT EVEREST

MOUNT ELBERT

The Rocky Mountains stretch for **4,800 km** through Canada and the United States. The highest peak is Mount Elbert at **4,401 m above sea level.**

The Great Plains are vast grasslands which cover **1,300,000 sq km** of the USA and Canada. Over **30 million bison** used to roam the Great Plains, but now only **541** remain.

The United States of America, Mexico and Canada make up North America. The music, television and film of the USA have a great influence on the rest of the world.

1,315,000,000 movie tickets sold in the USA and Canada in 2016

321,000,000 movie tickets sold in Mexico in 2016

MOVIE TICKETS

Over **3,000,000 US children** under **11** went to a movie in 2016

Over **5,000,000 US people** over **60** went to a movie in 2016

NUMBER OF MOVIE SCREENS

Canada 2,641

United States 43,531

Mexico 6,225

- Large bag of popcorn in 1930: **US 5 cents**
- Large bag of popcorn in 2016: **US$9**
  72,500,000 kg of ready-made popcorn sold in 2016
- Bag of popcorn at the 2017 National Football League Superbowl: **US$15**

MEXICAN FOOTBALL

Football is Mexico's favourite sport and Liga MX is its top league. **Over 4,249,470 people** went to see a Liga football match during the 2016–2017 football season.

NATIONAL SPORT

Canadians are passionate followers of ice hockey and go to matches at all levels – from high school tournaments to National Hockey League playoffs.

During the 2017–2018 season, **over 9,000,000 fans** attended NHL matches in Canada.

TELEVISION

Over **97.4% of American households** own at least **one** television set and **58% of households own two or more**. However, the number of households without a TV **doubled** between 2009 and 2016 as more consumers are using their smartphones, laptops and tablets to watch TV.

Total annual revenue made by US broadcasters: **US $148,000,000**

The average American watches **five hours** of TV every day.

'The Big Bang Theory' was the USA's favourite show in 2016, with **22.73 million viewers** per episode.

CBS is the leading US cable network with **8.8 million viewers** in 2016.

SHOPPING MALLS

Between 1956 and 2005, **1,500 malls were built** in the US. But now, hundreds are shutting as people opt to shop online. It is predicted that **a quarter of malls** in North America will shut by 2022. In Mexico, however, malls are thriving. In 2018, **34 new malls** were being built over with a total of **1.46 million sq metres** of retail space.

MALL COUNTDOWN

West Edmonton Mall in Alberta, Canada is the largest in North America and the **tenth largest** in the world, measuring **493,000 sq m**. It contains:

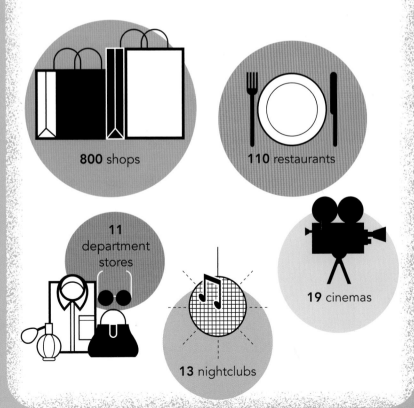

800 shops

110 restaurants

11 department stores

13 nightclubs

19 cinemas

17

11,770 MM OF RAIN FALL ON TUTUNENDO, COLOMBIA EVERY YEAR

There are **twelve countries** in South America and they share a range of different climates. These range from the steamy heat of rainforests to super-dry deserts, and the icy air of the snowy Andean mountains.

HOT AND COLD

The greatest extremes of temperature take place in Argentina. In 1907, the lowest temperature for South America of **-32.8°C** was recorded in the town of Sarmiento, central Argentina. South America's highest temperature of **48.9°C** was recorded in 1905 in the town of Rivadavia, northern Argentina.

Humans are not built for extreme heat or cold. Most people suffer hyperthermia (excess body heat) after **10 minutes** in **60°C heat**.

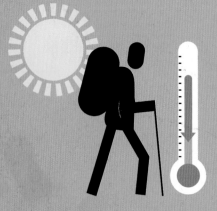

A person cannot live for long if their body temperature drops to **21°C** from its normal **37°C**.

HIGH AND LOW

Argentina has the highest and lowest geographical points in South America:

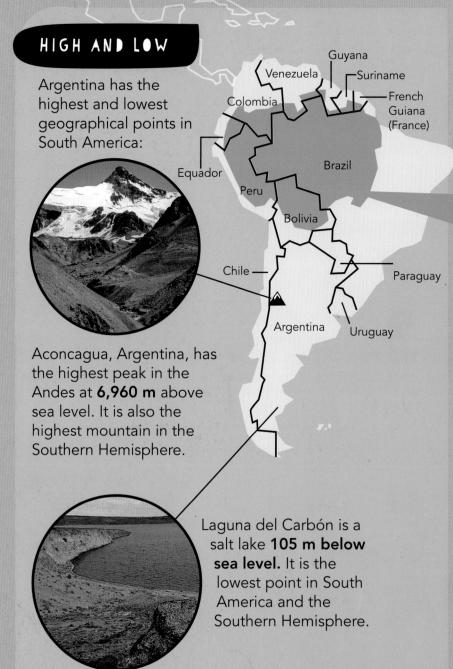

Aconcagua, Argentina, has the highest peak in the Andes at **6,960 m** above sea level. It is also the highest mountain in the Southern Hemisphere.

Laguna del Carbón is a salt lake **105 m below sea level.** It is the lowest point in South America and the Southern Hemisphere.

A salt lake is a lake found in a landlocked country that has **three or more grams of salt per every one litre of wate**r.

Guyana
Venezuela
Suriname
Colombia
French Guiana (France)
Equador
Brazil
Peru
Bolivia
Chile
Paraguay
Argentina
Uruguay

DRY AND WET

The driest place in South America is the Atacama Desert, Chile, which receives an average annual rainfall of **15 mm**. The wettest place in South America is Tutunendo in Colombia, where it rains an average of 11,770 mm a year.

Mawsynram, India: average annual rainfall: **11,871 mm**

Cherrapunji, India: average annual rainfall: **11,777 mm**

Tutunendo, Colombia: average annual rainfall: **11,770 mm**

THE AMAZON

The Amazon Rainforest stretches a massive **5,500,000 sq km** across Colombia, Peru, Venezuela, Ecuador, Bolivia, Guyana, Suriname and Brazil. It is the largest rainforest in the world with over **390 billion trees**.

AMAZON COUNTDOWN

The Amazon Rainforest is one of the most abundant habitats for life on Earth. Around **30% of all of the world's wildlife species** can be found there, including:

30,000,000 insects

40,000 plants

16,000 trees

5,600 fish

1,400 butterflies

1,300 birds

1,000 amphibians

427 mammals

400 reptiles

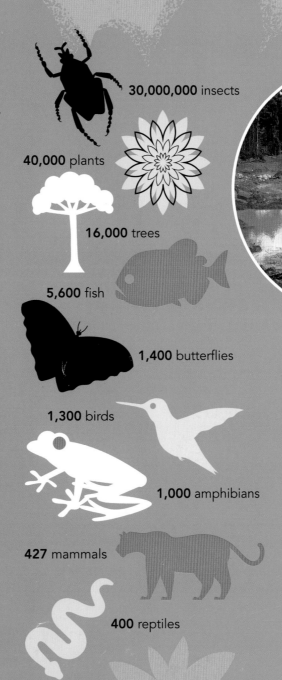

The world's rainforests covered **14% of the Earth's land surface 50 years ago**. Now they only cover **6%**. Every year, an area of rainforest the size of **8,571,295 football pitches** is lost to logging and farming.

THE RAILWAY LINE IN PERU CLIMBS TO A HEIGHT OF 4,818 M

South America does not have a connected transport system. Instead, people travel over land using a mixture of roads, railways and rivers. In total, the continent has over **100,000 km of railway tracks**.

Argentina's railway runs for a total length of **45,000 km**: it could wrap around the whole world.

RAILWAYS

Peru has **two** of the **five highest railway lines** in the world. The country's highest railway line climbs **4,818 m** via the city of Cerro de Pasco in the Andes. Peru's second highest railway line travels to the ruins of the ancient Inca city of Machu Picchu. It also stops at Lake Titicaca, the largest lake in South America and highest lake in the world, at **3,812 m above sea level**.

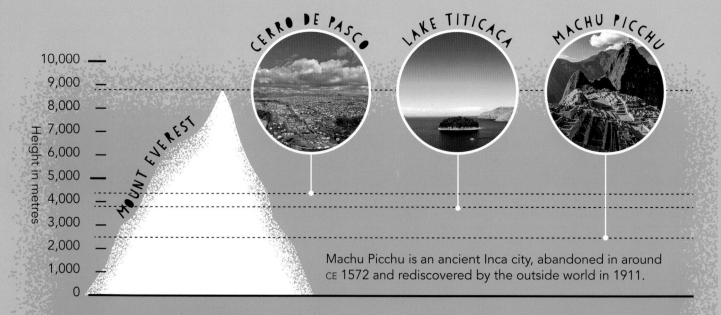

CERRO DE PASCO

LAKE TITICACA

MACHU PICCHU

MOUNT EVEREST

Height in metres

10,000
9,000
8,000
7,000
6,000
5,000
4,000
3,000
2,000
1,000
0

Machu Picchu is an ancient Inca city, abandoned in around CE 1572 and rediscovered by the outside world in 1911.

BOATS AND BARGES

Peru's railway line does not end at Lake Titicaca. Trains cross the lake aboard a barge and then continue their journey on the other side, in Bolivia. A more traditional lake transport are balsa boats made from totora reeds by the indigenous Uros people. Balsa boats vary in size from small, **one-person canoes** to **30-m-long ships**.

Balsa boat

RIVERS

The Amazon River provides one of the main transport highways in South America. At **6,400 km**, the Amazon is the **second longest river** in the world and it contains **20% of the world's river water**.

The Amazon Basin is a **7,500,000-square-km area** where the Amazon River and the smaller rivers coming off it lie. They provide **thousands of kilometres** of waterways for boats and ships.

Brazil's highways are **1,700,000 km in length** – more than **four times** the distance to the Moon and back.

ROADS

South America has an expanding network of roads. However, in many countries only some of the roads are paved and often too narrow for **two vehicles** to pass each other. The road network in Brazil is **1,700,000 km long**. However, sealed roads make up only **13% of the country's entire network**.

South America

AIRPORTS

Like South American roads, not all of the continent's airports have sealed runways. Brazil has **4,093 airports: 698 sealed and 3,395 unsealed**. However, air travel in South America is developing fast. In 2016, **over 185 million people** travelled by plane here. This high number was in part due to the Olympic Games being hosted on the continent.

In 2016, 10% of all new airports worldwide were built in South America.

Rest of the world

Antarctica is the only continent in the world without a country. It is also the coldest, driest and windiest continent in the world. As a result, there are no permanent residents in Antarctica. However, around **38,478 people** visit every year.

LAND

Antarctica has total land area of **13,829,430 sq km**. However, **98% of this land** is covered by an ice sheet with an average thickness of **2.45 km**. The continent also only receives a total rainfall of **200 mm a year**.

That's 90% of the world's ice.
Antarctica's ice sheet contains 29 million cubic kilometres of ice.

90%

ANTARCTICA   USA   AUSTRALIA   UK

Antarctica is **1.4 times bigger** than the USA; **1.8 times** bigger than Australia and **58 times** bigger than the UK.

MOUNT EVEREST

VINSON MASSIF

Vinson Massif is Antarctica's highest mountain at 4,897 m.

TEMPERATURE

In Antarctica, it is always cold. At the South Pole, the most southerly point on the planet, the average summer temperature is **-28°C**. In winter the average is **-60°C**. However the coldest temperature on Earth, **-89.2°C**, was recorded at the Vostok Station, **1,300 km** from the South Pole. Antarctica's strong winds make it colder still.

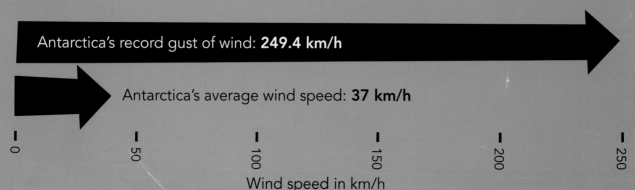

Antarctica's record gust of wind: **249.4 km/h**

Antarctica's average wind speed: **37 km/h**

0   50   100   150   200   250

Wind speed in km/h

POPULATION

Antarctica does not have any permanent human residents. Instead, scientists who work in the continent's **161 research stations** visit for a part of the year. Some tourists also land on Antarctica, but most visitors simply sail around its coast.

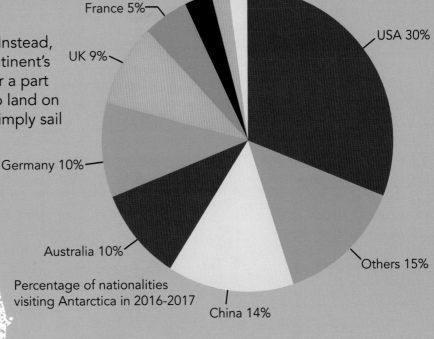

Switzerland 2%
Japan 2%
Canada 3%
France 5%
UK 9%
USA 30%
Germany 10%
Australia 10%
Others 15%
China 14%

Percentage of nationalities visiting Antarctica in 2016-2017

Around **4,400 people** move to Antarctica for the summer

Around **1,000 people** move to Antarctica for the winter

Around **13,000,000 penguins** live in Antarctica

CONSERVATION

Fifty-three countries have signed the Antarctic Treaty System which is designed to protect the continent. The treaty prohibits mining, military activity and the dumping of waste anywhere on Antarctica.

Despite winds that give the air a temperature of **-60°C**, the male emperor penguin spends **two months** standing on the ice to protect its unborn baby's egg until it hatches.

OVER 1,200 MUSEUMS AND ART GALLERIES IN FRANCE

Europe is the most popular destination for tourists in the world. Around **616,000,000 tourists** visit Europe every year. Its **50 countries** provide a wealth of culture, history and scenery.

MOST POPULAR COUNTRIES

The following most visited countries of Europe are also among the **top ten** tourist destinations in the world.

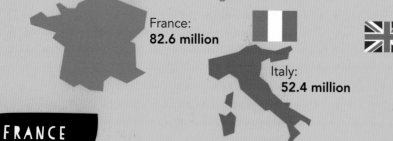

Spain:
75.6 million

France:
82.6 million

Italy:
52.4 million

United Kingdom:
35.8 million

Germany:
35.6 million

FRANCE

France tops the rankings for the **number one tourist destination** in the world. There are **over 1,200 museums and art galleries** in France; **more than 200 of them** are in its capital city, Paris.

MOST VISITED MUSEUMS AND ART GALLERIES

Louvre, Paris, France:
8.1 million

British Museum, London, UK:
5.9 million

State Hermitage Museum, St Petersburg:
4.2 million

Reina Sofía, Madrid, Spain:
3.8million

Galleria degli Uffizi, Florence, Italy:
2.2 million

SPAIN

Spain is well known for its food and many tourists are drawn to the country to sample its cuisine. Tapas are perhaps the best-known meal. Tapas are actually small snacks that were traditionally used as a lid to keep the flies out of a person's drink! Today, people order multiple tapas dishes to have as a meal.

COUNTING DOWN TAPAS

Tapas are usually a collection of food served on a small plate, such as:

12 olives

10 calamares, or battered squid rings

8 anchovies in vinegar

6 meatballs in sauce

1 tortilla, or Spanish omelette

ITALY

Italy was the centre of the ancient Roman Empire and the country is rich with the historical buildings left behind. This is especially true of the city of Rome. With around **10,000,000 tourists a year**, Rome is the **14th most visited city in the world**.

The Colosseum is Rome's **number one** tourist destination. Opened in CE 80, it attracts around **four million people every year**.

100,000 slaves built the Colosseum

Seating for **50,000 spectators**

11,000 wild animals at Emperor Trajan's games

Trajan's games lasted for **123 days** in a row

Top gladiator Flamma won **34 times** in the Colosseum

The Colosseum's original walls were **55 m high**

Although Europe is the **second smallest continent**, it is also the most densely populated. Over **742 million people** are crammed into **10,000,000 sq km**. That's **127 people per square km of land**.

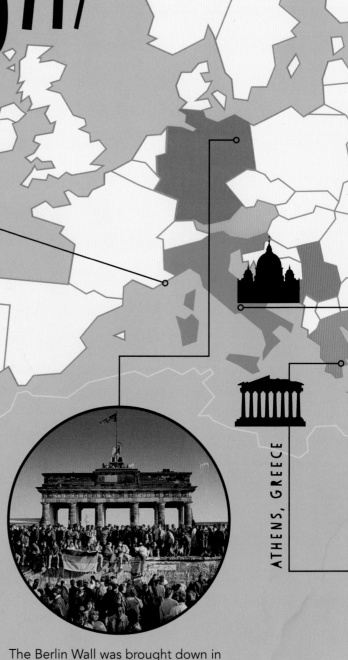

> I'M 89 YEARS OLD

People in Monaco have the highest life expectancy in the world at 89.7 years.

BORDERS

The people of Europe live in **50 countries**, many of which share a border with **two or more countries**. Over the centuries, these borders have often been redrawn in times of war and military expansion.

Russia:
14 neighbours

Germany:
9 neighbours

Serbia:
8 neighbours

Austria:
8 neighbours

ATHENS, GREECE

EAST AND WEST

After Germany was defeated in the Second World War the country was divided in **two**. Western Germany was ruled over by the Allied European countries and eastern Germany by the Soviet Union. A **155 km wall** in Berlin divided the country in two.

The Berlin Wall was brought down in 1989 when the country was reunified.

RUSSIA

Between 1945 and 1991, Russia led a group of communist countries called the Soviet Union. In 1991 the Soviet Union split into **15 separate countries**, including Russia. It is the largest country in the world at **17,100,000 sq km**. It stretches across the **two continents** of Europe and Asia. Around **23% of its territory** is in Europe; the rest is in Asia.

RUSSIA

The Vatican City would fit into Russia **38 million times**.

VATICAN CITY

The Vatican City is the smallest nation-state in Europe at **0.44 square km**. Situated in Rome, Italy, the Vatican is the centre of the Catholic Church and home of the Pope. Around **800 people** live in the Vatican City, but only **450** live there permanently.

EUROPEAN UNION

The European Union (EU) is a group of **27 countries** that share common political, economic and social policies. The EU was created to make Europe a more united place after the Second World War, Over **60 million people** were killed during the **six-year** war.

Greece is made up of a mainland and around **2,000 island**s. Only **170 of the islands** are populated.

Over **one third** of the world's wealth is located in Europe, making it the richest continent in the world.

AUSTRALIA IS THE ONLY CONTINENT WITH ONE COUNTRY

Australia is a continent, a country and a vast island in the south Pacific Ocean. Australia is also one of **10,000 islands** that make up Oceania. Oceania contains **14 different countries** and has a population of **40 million people**.

LAND AND SEA

The Pacific is the world's largest ocean at **161,000,000 sq km**. It is larger than all of the world's continents and islands combined. Most of the islands of Oceania dot this vast space.

Papua New Guinea

Nauru

Most of the land in Oceania is found in Australia, the region's largest country. New Zealand is the next largest. Only **4,840,470 people** live in New Zealand, compared to Australia's **24,754,000 people**.

Tasman Sea

New Zealand

New Zealand: **270,692 sq km**
Papua New Guinea: **462,840 sq km**
Other Oceanic countries: **89,268 sq km**

Australia: 7,692,202 sq km

A COASTAL STORY

New Zealand is **28 times smaller** than Australia, but it has more than **twice** the length of coastline with **15,000 km**, the **9th longest in the world**. At **107 km**, Ripiro Beach is the country's longest single beach.

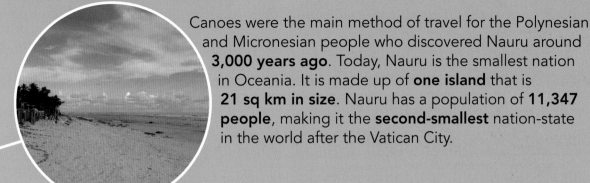

Canoes were the main method of travel for the Polynesian and Micronesian people who discovered Nauru around **3,000 years ago**. Today, Nauru is the smallest nation in Oceania. It is made up of **one island** that is **21 sq km in size**. Nauru has a population of **11,347 people**, making it the **second-smallest** nation-state in the world after the Vatican City.

Nauru is close to the equator so it stays warm all year round.
It has an average temperature of 30°C during the day and 25°C at night.

GREAT BARRIER REEF

The Great Barrier Reef is located off the coast of Australia and is the largest living structure in the world. It is made up of **billions of coral polyps**. Healthy coral polyps are covered in a colourful algae. However, global warming has led to rising sea temperatures, killing off the coral. When it dies, the algae falls off and only the bleached white coral skeleton remains.

COUNTING DOWN THE GREAT BARRIER REEF

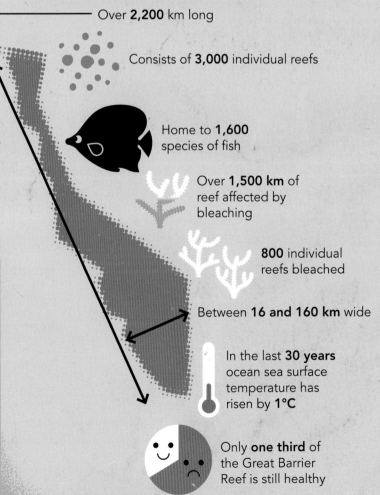

Over **2,200** km long

Consists of **3,000** individual reefs

Home to **1,600** species of fish

Over **1,500 km** of reef affected by bleaching

800 individual reefs bleached

Between **16 and 160 km** wide

In the last **30 years** ocean sea surface temperature has risen by **1°C**

Only **one third** of the Great Barrier Reef is still healthy

Ripiro Beach is the site of over **113 shipwrecks**.

FURTHER INFORMATION

BOOKS

Big Countdown: Planet Earth by Paul Rockett (Franklin Watts, 2016)
How to Build Your Own Country by Valerie Wyatt (Wayland, 2015)
The Land and the People: Japan by Susie Brooks (Wayland, 2018)

WEBSITES

A kid-friendly website that provides information, trivia and fun facts about the countries of the world.
www.sciencekids.co.nz/sciencefacts/countries.html
This National Geographic website invites kids to 'explore the world', including regions that need protection from climate change.
www.natgeokids.com/uk/?s=explore+the+world
This NASA website gives stunning live video footage of the Earth from the International Space Station's cameras:
www.ustream.tv/channel/iss-hdev-payload

Note to parents and teachers:
Every effort has been made by the publisher to ensure that these websites contain no inappropriate or offensive material. However, because of the nature of the Internet, it is impossible to guarantee that the content of these sites will not be altered. We strongly advise that Internet access is supervised by a responsible adult.

LARGE NUMBERS

1,000,000,000,000,000,000,000,000,000,000,000 = ONE DECILLION
1,000,000,000,000,000,000,000,000,000,000 = ONE NONILLION
1,000,000,000,000,000,000,000,000,000 = ONE OCTILLION
1,000,000,000,000,000,000,000,000 = ONE SEPTILLION
1,000,000,000,000,000,000,000 = ONE SEXTILLION
1,000,000,000,000,000,000 = ONE QUINTILLION
1,000,000,000,000,000 = ONE QUADRILLION
1,000,000,000,000 = ONE TRILLION
1,000,000,000 = ONE BILLION
1,000,000 = ONE MILLION
1000 = ONE THOUSAND
100 = ONE HUNDRED
10 = TEN
1 = ONE

GLOSSARY

abundance	a large quantity of something
broadcaster	an organisation that transmits radio or television programmes
canyon	a deep valley with steep sides, usually with a river flowing through it
carat	a unit of weight for precious stones, such as diamonds
consumer	a person who buys goods and services
culture	the arts, beliefs and social practices of a group of people
cuisine	the style of cooking associated with a particular country or group of people
descendant	a person that is descended from an ancestor
dialect	the way a language is used by a particular regional group
economy	the way an economic system in a country is arranged
endangered	a species that is at risk of extinction
exporter	a person, country or company that sends goods or services somewhere else for sale
exploit	to get value from something
gorge	a narrow valley between hills or mountain
hyperthermia	a medical condition when the body's temperature becomes higher than normal
Inca	A South American people who lived around Peru between the 13th and 16th centuries
industrial revolution	the rapid development of machinery to bring about change in a country's economy
landlocked	enclosed by land
landmass	a large area of land
mall	a large enclosed shopping area that people can walk around
mammal	a warm-blooded animal that has fur and feeds its young milk
megacity	a large city with a population of over 10 million people
megafauna	large animals that weigh over 40 kg
migrate	to move from one place to another to find better conditions
mineral	a solid organic substance obtained by mining, such as diamonds
nectar	a sweet liquid which is secreted by plants
pasture	land or a plot of grassland that animals graze on
pipeline	a long-distance pipe that delivers substances such as oil
population	the number of people in a place
poacher	someone who illegally kills animals for profit
reed	a thin, flexible strip of wood
resource	something that is found in nature that humans can use, such as minerals, water, a forest
renewable	something that can be used and then replaced, such as grassland
replica	an exact copy of something
rural	in the countryside
sealed road	a road with a hard surface made of concrete or tarmac
smog	a thick haze caused by polluted air
treaty	an agreement between states, countries or rulers
tundra	a large, treeless area in the Arctic where the ground remains permanently frozen
urban	area in a city
venomous	having or containing venom

INDEX